DATE DUE

363.72   BC#34880000025218 $25.36
GAL   Galko, Francine
          Earth friends at home

Morrill E.S.
Chicago Public Schools
1431 North Leamington Avenue
Chicago, IL 60651

Earth Friends at Home

Francine Galko

Heinemann Library
Chicago, Illinois

© 2004 Heinemann Library
a division of Reed Elsevier Inc.
Chicago, Illinois

Customer Service 888-454-2279

Visit our website at www.heinemannlibrary.com

Designed by Anna Matras/Heinemann Library
Illustration by Carrie Gowran
Photo research by Heather Sabel
Printed and bound in China
by South China Printing Company Limited

08 07 06 05
10 9 8 7 6 5 4 3 2

**Library of Congress
Cataloging-in-Publication Data**
Galko, Francine.
  Earth friends at home / Francine Galko.
  p. cm. -- (Earth friends)
  Summary: Discusses the importance of reducing
waste, recycling, and reusing products in the context
of life at home.
  Includes bibliographical references and index.
  ISBN 1-4034-4895-7 (library binding-hardcover) --
ISBN 1-4034-4900-7 (pbk.)
  1. Environmental protection--Citizen participation--
Juvenile literature. 2. Energy conservation--Juvenile
literature. 3. Recycling (Waste, etc.)--Juvenile
literature. [1. Environmental protection--Citizen
participation. 2. Energy conservation. 3. Recycling
(Waste)] I. Title.
  TD171.7.G3495 2004
  363.72'8--dc22   2003021007

Acknowledgments
The author and publisher are grateful to the
following for permission to reproduce copyright
material: p. 4 Corbis; pp. 5, 6, 10, 14, 16, 18, 19, 25,
26, 27, 28, 29, 30 Greg Williams/ Heinemann
Library; pp. 8, 12, 13, 20, 22, 23, 24 Jill Birschbach/
Heinemann Library; p. 9 Ken Graham/Getty Images;
p. 11 Lon C. Diehl/PhotoEdit Inc.; p. 15 Photodisc/
Getty Images; p. 17 Steven Lunetta/PhotoEdit Inc.;
p. 21 Richard Hamilton/Corbis

Cover photo by Greg Williams/Heinemann Library

Every effort has been made to contact copyright
holders of any material reproduced in this book.
Any omissions will be rectified in subsequent
printings if notice is given to the publisher.

Some words are shown in bold, **like this.** You can find out what they mean by looking in the glossary.

To learn about the picture on the front cover, turn to page 5.

Contents

What Is an Earth Friend? 4

Reduce, Reuse, and Recycle 6

Water in Your Home 8

Using Less Water in the Bathroom 10

Washing Dishes 12

Energy in Your Home 14

Saving Energy at Home 16

Keeping Your Home Comfortable 18

Garbage, Garbage Everywhere 20

Making Less Garbage 22

Reusing Things in Your Home 24

Recycling at Home 26

Using Less Paper 28

Activity: Make a Watering Can 30

Glossary 31

More Books to Read 32

Index 32

What Is an Earth Friend?

Earth friends use **natural resources** carefully. Natural resources are important **materials** found in nature. They include the air we breathe and the water we drink. Land and trees are also natural resources.

This boy is putting an **aluminum** can in the **recycling** bin.

Earth friends use only what they need.
They do not waste natural resources.
Earth friends also help keep Earth clean.

Reduce, Reuse, and Recycle

When you use **natural resources,** use as little as you can. For example, turn off the lights when you leave a room. This **reduces** the amount of energy you use.

Reuse and **recycle** things when you can. Glass and plastic can often be recycled. You can reuse cloth napkins, but paper napkins have to be thrown away.

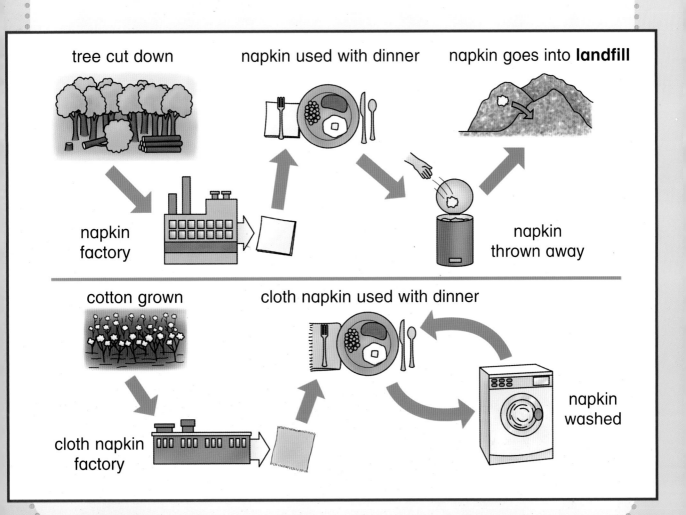

tree cut down

napkin used with dinner

napkin goes into **landfill**

napkin factory

napkin thrown away

cotton grown

cloth napkin used with dinner

cloth napkin factory

napkin washed

Water in Your Home

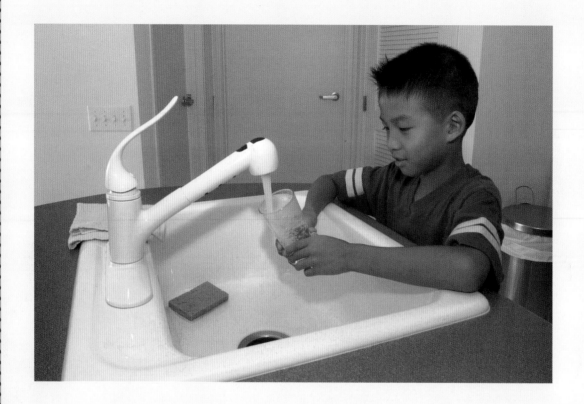

When you turn on the water **faucet** at home, clean water comes out. The water might come from a river or lake. Drinking water also comes from deep in the ground.

People use a lot of water. But there is only so much clean water in the ground, lakes, and rivers. If we waste water or **pollute** it, we could run out.

Using Less Water in the Bathroom

This boy is saving water by turning off the **faucet** while he brushes his teeth.

Do not let the water run. You can waste about two milk jugs of water while you brush your teeth. Just wet your toothbrush, then turn off the water until it is time to rinse.

Long showers and deep baths use a lot of water. Take quick showers or a **shallow** bath. You can turn off the water in the shower while you soap up.

Washing Dishes

When you wash the dishes, do not let the water run. Fill the sink with soapy water and wash the dishes. Then fill the sink with clean water for rinsing.

Dishwashers use a lot of water. Most dishwashers use the same amount of water whether they are full or not. Turn the dishwasher on only when it is full.

Energy in Your Home

These children are using electric lights, a television, and a video game player.

Many things in your home need **electricity** to work. Electricity comes mostly from burning **fossil fuels. Gasoline** and oil are fossil fuels.

Fossil fuels are found deep inside Earth. It took a very long time for them to form. Once they are used up, fossil fuels will be gone. When we **conserve** electricity, we use less fossil fuel.

Saving Energy at Home

This girl is turning off the television.

Turn off things that use **electricity** when you are not using them. When you leave a room, turn off the lights.

The refrigerator uses electricity to keep food cool. When the refrigerator door is open, warm air gets inside. Decide what you want before you open the refrigerator.

Keeping Your
Home Comfortable

Close the door when you enter and leave
your home. If you leave the door open, the
heater or **air conditioner** uses more energy.

Close shades, blinds, and curtains on hot, sunny days. This helps keep your home cool in summer. Shades, blinds, and curtains also keep the air inside your house warmer during winter.

Garbage, Garbage Everywhere

What happens to the things you put in the garbage can? Some of it is taken to a **landfill.** A landfill is a big hole in the ground for garbage.

Some things you put in the garbage can go to a landfill like this one.

Some garbage is burned in big **incinerators.**

Other things in your garbage will be burned. Burning garbage puts dirt into the air. The less garbage you make, the cleaner Earth will be.

Making Less Garbage

Buy **containers** that can be **reused.**
For example, do not buy yogurt in small
containers. One large yogurt container
makes less garbage.

You can also buy cereal in a large box.
One large box does not make much garbage.
Small boxes of cereal make a lot more garbage.

Reusing Things in Your Home

wooden cookie jar

When you use **reuse** things, you do not throw them away as fast. You do not make as much garbage. For example, store food in **containers** you can clean and use again.

You can use **plastic** milk jugs to make many useful things for your home. This girl has made a watering can from a milk jug.

To see how you can make a watering can like this one, turn to page 30.

25

Recycling at Home

aluminum cans

Things that are **recycled** can be used to make new things. For example, used **aluminum** cans can be made into new drink cans.

You can also recycle newspapers, glass **containers,** and some **plastic** bottles. Keep these things out of the garbage can. Help your family save them for recycling.

Using Less Paper

Use both sides of the paper when you write or draw. You can also **reuse** some paper in computer printers. After you use both sides of the paper, **recycle** it.

You can sort used paper so that it is easy to reuse.

Do not use paper towels. Sponges and cloth rags are good for cleaning up messes. Sponges and cloth rags can be reused.

Activity:
Make a Watering Can

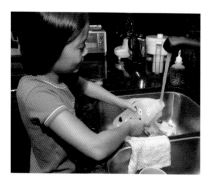

1. Find an old plastic milk or water jug and rinse it out.

2. Have an adult help you use scissors to punch five to ten holes near the top of the bottle.

3. Decorate your new watering can with stickers or markers.

4. Fill the jug with water and give your plants a drink.

Glossary

air conditioner   machine that makes air cooler

aluminum   kind of light metal

conserve   use less of a natural resource

container   box or bottle used to hold something

dishwasher   machine that cleans dishes

electricity   energy that powers things like radios and lights

faucet   metal knob that controls the flow of water in a sink

fossil fuel   oil, coal, or natural gas

gasoline   liquid fuel used to power cars and other machines

incinerator   machine that burns garbage

landfill   place where garbage is buried

material   what a thing is made of

natural resource   important material found in nature

plastic   material made from coal or oil, water, and a kind of rock

pollute   put harmful materials into the air, water, or ground

recycle   collect materials so they can be used again

reduce   use or make less

reuse   use again

shallow   not deep

More Books to Read

McHarry, Jan. *The Great Recycling Adventure.* Atlanta: Turner Publishing, 1996.

Oxlade, Chris. *Paper.* Chicago: Heinemann Library, 2001.

Oxlade, Chris. Water. Chicago: Heinemann Library, 2002.

Royston, Angela. *Recycling.* Austin, Tex.: Raintree Publishers, 1999.

Index

air conditioners 18

bathroom 10–11

containers 7, 22–23, 24, 26, 27

electricity 14–15, 16–17

fossil fuels 14, 15

garbage 20–21, 22, 23, 24, 27

materials 4

natural resources 4, 5, 6

paper 7, 28–29

recycling 5, 7, 26–27, 28
reducing 6
reusing 7, 22, 24–25, 28, 29

washing dishes 12–13
water 4, 8–9, 10–11, 12–13